drawn
BY HIS
hand

"an illustrated
devotional to
draw you
CLOSER TO
God!"

PUBLISHED BY www.createspace.com
ISBN 13: 978-1503198371
ISBN 10: 1503198375

♥ table of contents ♥

Welcome!
what you hold in your hands is

a piece of heart

almost 10 years in the making.
It was 2004 when i first
sensed God placing the inspiration for these drawings
in my spirit.

This collection of drawings
is called "drawn by His hand"
because that's what they are!
Inspiration given by God;
each Picture drawn to draw
you into closer relationship
with Him. Indeed anyone
who comes into a relationship

with the Lord is surely
"drawn by His hand."

Through the years God has
used these drawings count-
less times to encourage
me in His Word. I am thankful
for the fun & important part
of my life they have been. I
believe they will encourage you
as they have encouraged me.

While each picture was drawn
with an excellence of heart
and a sincere desire to bless
you, what you won't find here
is perfection. It was of higher
importance for me to share
these drawings than to be

perfect. In fact, i encourage you to do the same - share your "God colors"; no perfection required. As you make your way through this book, let your inspiration & imperfection soar! Take the time to enjoy each drawing, meditate on the verses, listen to what Holy Spirit is saying, add your own doodles to each page, take a nap, drink a mocha, read some more and on & on... this is your journey.

Praise be to Father, Son & Holy Ghost as we are drawn by His hand. in love, Anne

dedicated to

GOD,

christopher
& Harvey ♥

...GOOD NEWS...

You know the feeling you get when you walk to the mailbox? A sense of anticipation that somehow today is the day that some amazingly good news has found it's way to you?!

You know the feeling when you open up your mailbox and the only thing in there is bills?

- Well have i got
- GOOD NEWS for you!

Everyday for each & every person who has confessed Jesus as Lord and believed God raised Him from the dead (Romans 10:9) is a GOOD NEWS day! Yahoo!

2

At the moment of our salvation we are absolved from every charge. The charges (our sins) are gone, erased, goodbye & adios! To be absolved means "to free from guilt or blame." As a believer, Jesus took our guilt and blame upon Himself as He died for our sins on the cross.

We are free!

The NKJV says we are "justified" which means to "Put us back where we ought to have been." With Jesus our relationship with God is restored - it is Put right back where it ought to have been - a relationship of love, intimacy, trust and more!

A word of warning: the devil tries hard to condemn us for any and every sin we've ever committed. He wants to smother us in the guilt & blame that Christ freed us from. But take heart, God's Word promises that there is no condemnation for those who belong to Christ Jesus (Romans 8:1). Certainly this is no excuse to sin - we always want to be led by the Spirit of God & quick to repent when we sin - but in the meantime let's raise our hands in Praise, smile big and enjoy our freedom in Jesus! Our "bills" have been Paid and that, my friends, is GOOD NEWS!

PAID

"So we are Christ's ambassadors, God making His appeal as it were through us."
2 Corinthians 5:20a AMP

AB"
2014

...here's my card...

What do you do for a living?
What job have you signed
up for? Homemaker? Dr.?
Sales? Student? Artist?
Baker? Barista? Retired?

Have you ever thought about
the fact that besides "what
you do" or the job you go to
on a daily basis, as a believer
in Christ there's an added
dimension to each & every
moment of your day?

"We are Christ's
    AMBASSADORS,
God making His appeal
as it were through us."
1 corinthians 5:20 AMP

6

Everywhere you go, everything you do, you are representing Christ. This is a HOLY CALL!

Think about it. You're not just making the perfect cup of coffee for your customer; you're using the opportunity to serve others and going the extra mile to bless them. You're not just cleaning house & cooking meals, you're centering the heart of your home around Christ and making it a warm place for everyone who enters. You're not just going to school counting the days to summer break; you're helping your classmates succeed and cheering them on everyday.

Take what you do in the natural (job, career, position) and make it SUPERNATURAL by inviting Christ into each & every moment.

To be an ambassador means to be an authorized messenger or representative. God has authorized you in Christ to share His LOVE with the world, preach the GOSPEL and make DISCIPLES. You are Christ's ambassador today...now...in this very moment.

Think about that the next time someone asks you what you do for a living! God Bless!

no matter what shoes we're wearing...

"The steps of a [good] man are directed and established by the Lord when He delights in his way [and He busies Himself with his every step]" Psalm 37:23 AMP

... our every step ...

Did you catch that? Sure the bunny slippers are comfy and cute 🐰. Yes the high heels look ≷SNAZZY≷. But let me ask you again...did you catch that??

" THE STEPS OF A [GOOD] MAN are DIRECTED & ESTABLISHED BY THE LORD WHEN HE DELIGHTS IN HIS WAY [AND HE BUSIES HIMSELF WITH HIS EVERY STEP]. "

EVERY STEP.

Pause & think about that for a moment with me, will you?

There's not one step that you or i will take today where the Lord won't be with us. Not a single solitary step He won't notice. Not one moment where He won't be with you, by your side, rooting you on into a deeper level of holiness and delighting in your steps as you follow His lead.

(wow, this realization is really convicting me as i write this and calling me on to holier living ... where have i been today? what have i said today? Have i realized every step is holy?)

Sidenote from Anne...

fill in the shoes with the places you must go today...

...and thank God He's with us every step!

Knowing that Jesus is with us
every step of our day is not only
a comfort but also a CALL
- a call to holier living.

→ a call to watch where we
   Step & make every move count
→ a call to strive each moment
   to Walk in His ways
→ a call to be His very Feet
   on the face of the earth
   shod in the gospel of peace
                    (see Ephesians 6:15)

So, bunny slippers, high heels
or the most ballin' pair of kicks
ever - let's get moving and
delight in the fact that He
delights in us! Every Step!

how does your garden grow?

"May you be rooted deep in, LoVe..."

ephesians 3:17b amp

AB° 2014

...the fruit at the root...

I have to admit for awhile i thought i had drawn this picture incorrectly and planned on changing it. The verse is talking about being rooted in love, yet this picture shows a bloom of love. Hmmmmm...

Then it dawned on me; the picture isn't wrong at all. You see, when we're rooted deep in love, LOVE is what's going to GROW, BLOSSOM and FRUIT in our lives.

Walking in love (a fruit of the Spirit) is a direct & natural result of being rooted in God's love. "the fruit begins at the root!"

What does it mean to
be rooted deep in love?

Well, just go out to your garden
and do a little experiment. Go
ahead and give a tug on a few
different flowers & weeds.

❀ Which ones pulled up easily?

❀ Which ones required an
        extra pull?

❀ Which ones are still there
  ↗ because they were rooted deep?

That's who believers are called
to be - those flowers that are
so deeply rooted in God's love
that even a good strong "tug"
from the circumstances of
life <u>can not</u> & <u>will not</u> uproot

us because we are firmly
established & fixed in Him.
We root ourselves in God's
love by:

♥ spending quiet
time with Him

♥ reading His
Word

♥ listening to
Holy Spirit

♥ Praise &
worship

♥ Meditating on
His Word

♥ Praying in
tongues

what other ways can we root ourselves in His love?

write your answers in the flower

What 1 thing will you do today to deeply root yourself in Him?

" And all these blessings shall come upon you and overtake you if you heed the voice of the Lord your God." deuteronomy 28:2 AMP

...heads or tails...

Heads or tails, you choose. No, not the flipping of a coin but, the literal head or tail. Do you want to be the head, the front, the beginning of something good? Or the tail, the stump, the south side of a donkey going north?

Not really a tough choice, is it?

Deuteronomy 19:30 tells us that God has put the decision in our hands.

"I have set before you life and death, the blessings and the curses; therefore choose life..."

Again, not really a tough
decision is it?

You see, when we choose to
believe the gospel truth about
Jesus Christ, wonderful things
happen. Not only are our sins
washed away and we receive
the eternal life of God but in
Christ we become qualified to
receive all of God's blessings.

How do we become qualified
to receive all of God's blessings?

in Christ.

I believe it blesses God when we
believe & receive His blessings.
Just like an earthly parent who

19

enjoys seeing their child delight in a gift they have given them — i believe God delights to see us walking in His blessings.

"blessed shall you be in the city and blessed shall you be in the field"

"blessed shall be the fruit of your body, the fruit of your ground and the fruit of your beasts"

"blessed shall be your storehouse and all you undertake"

That's a lot of blessings and they're all available to us now in Christ. Remember, heads or tails...it's your choice.

...thought makeover...

For real, let me ask you a question. When was the last time heaven filled your thoughts? Seriously, have you even thought about heaven lately? Short of funerals, movies or t.v. shows that tend to make us think about heaven, when was the last time you grabbed ahold of your mind and directed it towards heaven and all it's GLORY? Kind of crazy, huh?

Sitting here thinking about all the wordly things that vie for our attention boggles my mind.

So-called beauty magazines, weight loss & make-up ads,

car commercials, home improvement projects - all of these have empty promises attached to them that our lives will somehow be better if we make them a part of it - while heaven and it's glory sit ever waiting to reveal it's

Magnificence

to each one of us. So i ask again,

"Have you thought about heaven lately?"

Have you thought about who you'll see there? Thought about those you still need to share the gospel with? Thought about declaring heavenly blessings over your earthly life?

thought about those you're praying for? Thought about storing up your treasures in heaven? (Matthew 6:20) Thought about the majesty of the throne room? Thought about being in the presence of Jesus? Lots to think about huh?

No glossy paged empty promises here. Rather, a Savior who loves you & an eternity with Him.

Let heaven fill your thoughts today! Fill in the thought bubble with all the amazing things you're looking forward to in heaven.

master
holy holy

OMEGA

Lord of Lords

savior

healer
beautiful

wonderful

Shalom

JESUS

Lover

AB 2014

King of Kings

magnificent

Who or what are you magnifying in your life?

"Oh, magnify the Lord with me...
...let us exalt His name, PSALM together." 34:3
NKJV

. . . make Him big . . .

What have you made

BiG

in your life today?

Have you talked more about your problems or more about your God? More about what seems wrong with the world or more about how Right God is?

The AMAZING truth is God is on the throne and He has been established from all eternity (see Psalm 93:3).

The wisest action we can take for our lives is to humbly submit unto doing life this way.

The more we **magnify God, glorify Him** and allow Him to be Lord over EVERY aspect & area of our lives, the more our lives will be **divinely aligned** with His plans & purposes for us.

Magnifying God helps us keep our lives in proper perspective. God <u>first</u> and everything else <u>second</u>!

Let's play a game of
"Would You Rather?"

→ would you rather bask &
fellowship in the glory of God
... or wallow in the troubles
  of the day?

→ would you rather magnify
God so much that your problem diminishes ... or magnify
your problem so much that
  your view of God diminishes?

Tough decision?

I don't think so!

Make God B I G
in your life today!

what's 1 thing you can do to magnify God right now?

"Because YOUR loving-
kindness is better than life
my lips shall PRAISE YOU."

PSALM 63:3 amp

...not just lip service...

We can do a lot of great things with our lips. We can kiss a loved one. Eat lots of dark chocolate. Give a compliment. Eat more dark chocolate.

You catch my drift?

All joking aside, this verse just inherently makes me happy.☺ because doing something great for God is as close as our own two lips 👄.(No training required. No shipping & handling.)

The directive is simple:

1) OPEN MOUTH

2) RELEASE A PRAISE (ie JOYFUL NOISE, SHOUT, WAHOO etc.)

30

Imagine it... our two simple lips, something we probably take for granted everyday, being set apart and used for His holy purposes.

We can praise His name. Commend Him among the nations (starting with our family, friends, coworkers...) Preach the gospel & share our testimony.

We can sing a song, give a triumphant shout or declare His Word... and all of this can be done today, right now, right where we are.

Let's not overcomplicate this !!!

We all desire to make a
difference for His Kingdom
and in that moment when
we open our mouth and give
Him a

faith-filled Praise,

an eternal impact has been made.
#yesitsreallythatsimple
#yesireallymeanit
#dontholdback
Our mouths are holy
instruments used in
God's kingdom come
& His will being done
on earth today. Sign
me up! fill the lips
with the good things
of God that you'll share with others!

...extreme makeover...

You've seen them before, right?
The reality shows where participants sign up to receive a
makeover including hair, war-
drobe, weight & more? While i
never got too much into this
type of reality show, (a certain
show with castaways is my fave!)
my favorite part was seeing
the before & after shots of the
the makeover participants. It
was fun to see the changes
that had been made. Sometimes
there was hardly a difference
but sometimes the change was
so dramatic it looked like a
brand new person.

Well, guess what?!!

THAT'S WHAT GOD'S WORD DOES for US!

It gives us an extreme makeover into the mega-powered, supercharged, cape wearing superheroes we always knew we were. Ok, so maybe i'm exaggerating a bit here (after all, i don't own a cape)...but what God's Word does do is release His : POWER : over our lives as we declare it from our mouths.

"Death and life are in the power of the tongue..."
Proverbs 18:21 AMP

After all, who would you come after if you were the super-villain of the day? The weapon toting Word-covered warrior or the defenseless onlooker?

⁚ GET IN THE GAME ! ⁚

We have an enemy. He comes to kill, steal & destroy. (John 10:10) yet God has given us mighty weapons to use. (2 Corinthians 10:4) We can effect the very atmosphere of our lives by speaking God's Word. Wield your weapon and actively speak God's Word everyday! which verse will you add to your arsenal today?

write it here ↵

...the Lord's Prescription...

I've heard it said that the very best thing we can do is believe God's very best. (sure, im the one who said that but hey, i really do believe it)

As believers, we have been given the mind of Christ are are to constantly remind ourselves of all the good things of God.

In fact, Psalm 103:2* tells us,

"...forget not [one of] all His benefits..."

Another way of saying this is, "keep on reminding yourself of all God's promises, blessings & rewards." Oh the amazing promises for us in Jesus Christ!

*amplified translation 38

Let's take a moment right now
and stir ourselves up in the
HEALING PROMISES of the
Lord. Know someone who
needs a healing? Here's just
what the Dr. (aka Great Physician) ordered:

- "He sent out His word
  and healed them..." Psalm
  107:20a NLT

- "...by His wounds we are
  healed." Isaiah
  53:5b NIV

- "There shall be no evil befall
  you, nor any plague or ca-
  lamity come near your tent."
  PSALM 91:10AMP

- "He forgives all my sins
  and heals all my diseases."
  PSALM 103:3 NLT

You know, i've heard the gospel & the promises of God referred to as the "gos-pills" because they bring supernatural health & healing just like a pill does in the natural.

What other promises, blessings, rewards & "gos-pills" do you proclaim over your life?

Write them on the "prescrip- tion" sheet below. ———

from the Office of: _____
prescribed for: _____
_____
_____
_____

take one daily ☑ as directed by Holy Spirit ☑

do you ever see a love letter from God in the clouds?

"The heavens declare the glory of God; the skies proclaim the work of His hands." PSALM 19:1 NIV

...show me your glory...

Have you ever asked God to show you His glory? I have many times - desperate to see His face, wondering where He was, wanting to see evidence of Him in my day to day life - but that all changed one day as God ministered this verse to my ♥.

I was driving in the car longing to see God's face, asking Him to show me His glory, when all of a sudden this very verse popped right up in my spirit!

> " the heavens declare
>   the glory of God;
>   the skies proclaim
>   the work of His hands."
>   Psalm 19:1 NIV

It was a beautiful sunny day
with blue skies and a few white
fluffy clouds here & there and
that's when i got it!

God's glory is
already on display

He's showing us new aspects
of His beauty & glory everyday... the real question is,
"Are we receiving it?"

You see, as i ponder this more & more i wonder whether i've taken too much of His glory for granted. (i quickly realize the answer is yes)

..freshly budding spring flowers
sunrises to sunsets
the laughter of a loved one...

HIS GLORY IS ALREADY ON DISPLAY!

Sure, what we see here is only a glimpse of what's to come, but, since we're here now, i pray God gives me eyes to see and a spirit to receive His glory everyday.

take a look at the sky at different times today to draw what you see here

44

... TiGHt GriP...

This verse is very near & dear
to my heart as it is one of the
very first "Drawn by His Hand"
insights that God ever gave to me.

...a young girl held so tightly
in her loving Father's hand
that He most assuredly would
never let her go - not even
loosen His grip in the slightest.

♡   ♡   ♥   ♥   ♡   ♥

...a loving Father so enamored
with and caring towards our
lives that He emphatically
assures us 3 times that He
will not in any degree leave
us helpless nor let us down.

. . . a young girl, a young boy, a grown man, an elderly woman . . . whatever phase of life you're in right now, the facts don't change . . . God is for us (romans 8:31) and He cares for us (1 peter 5:7).

∹ let's imagine ∹ ⤳ Go ahead, close your eyes and believe & receive it. See yourself as that precious child held lovingly in God's grip.

1. HOW DOES iT FEEL TO BE SO ADORED?

2. HOW DOES iT FEEL TO BE SO CARED FOR?

write your answers here!

can YOU FEEL YOUR spirit LIFTING AS YOUR CARES? MELT AWAY in HIS HANDS!

God has used this particular drawing to minister to me numerous times since i first drew it. By His **grace** in those times when i felt most alone & most hopeless, this picture would pop into my spirit. **YAY!** At those times i was once again assured that i was...

He loves us! this much

→ never alone.
→ never abandoned
→ never without hope

...and neither are you!

We are lovingly held by a Father who is **truly, madly** & **deeply** in love with us: Yes, He really does love us that much! Amen!

...even on "those" days...

ok sure, yes Mr. Happy Heart and Rejoicing Tongue are cute little buggers but don't let them fool you - they are POWERFUL WEAPONS! (spiritual ninjas perhaps?)

You see, it's easy to Praise God on those once in a lifetime perfect days when everything goes our way but, what about "those" days when we wake up feeling like a mama grizzly who's mad at the world?

exhibit 1

Ever had one of "those" days? (or weeks, months or years?)

Having one today?

If so, then i've got great news for you!

50

THIS VERSE IS GOING TO STRENGTHEN US THE MOST; INDEED CHANGE OUR VERY CHARACTER THE _VERY_ MOST ON ONE OF "THOSE" DAYS

...because when we choose to live by God's Word rather than the circumstances around us or the feelings inside of us, OUR VERY SPIRIT IS STRENGTHENED!!!

When you can declare in faith that your heart is **GLAD** & your tongue **rejoices** -even in the midst of a "bad" day - then you know you've brought your "A GAME!"

It's like working out - your muscles grow the most when there's resistance. Spiritually speaking, one of "those" days is the perfect opportunity to hit the (spiritual) gym.

So, go ahead...put on your party hat and get to rejoicing in the Lord!

-even if you're having one of "those" days.

fill in the party hats with all the reasons to rejoice

♥∽ salvation invitation ∽

Maybe you feel a stirring or a softness in your heart that's never been there before... for me it was like my insides broke into pieces & i knew i was being rearranged/recreated.

"Today, if you will hear His voice: "Do not harden your hearts"...
PSALM 95:7 NKJV

"Indeed, the "right time" is now. Today is the day of salvation."
2 Corinthians 6:26 NLT

"Everyone who calls on the name of the Lord will be saved."
Romans 10:13 NLT

Pray: "Father I declare, "Jesus is Lord!" I believe He died for the forgiveness of my sins and you raised Him from the dead. Thank you that i am a new creation in Christ and Holy Spirit is my forever guide. Thank you for loving me. I love you too. Amen.

36906732R00035

Made in the USA
Charleston, SC
17 December 2014